COPING

WITH

ADOPTION

Maya Thomas

COPING WITH ADOPTION

Book and Cover design by Norbert Elnar
Interior Design by Joy Bradford, ISBN: 978-1-948581-77-6

First Edition: November 2020

DEDICATION

This book is dedicated to my beautiful son
Elijah Malachi Thomas

CONTENTS

Preface

Maya Thomas prefaces **Coping with Adoption**. This memoir reflects on me being a teenage mom and how putting my son up for adoption changed my life. I talk about the shame and feelings of defeat that made me question my entire being. I hope my story helps others who have experienced a similar journey find comfort in knowing they are not alone. For those who have never experienced anything like this, I hope to enlighten them.

MAYA THOMAS

COPING WITH ADOPTION

Part I

COPING WITH ADOPTION

1

INTENTIONS BEHIND TELLING MY STORY

A lot of my book can appear to be a bashing session where I am blaming everyone else for what happened. That is very far from the truth different events and people played a role in my situation, which led to the outcomes that manifested. The major outcome that has molded and shaped me was the story of my son's adoption. This monumental time in my life is something that I feel can aid others in their personal healing processes if they can relate to my journey. I also would like for my experience to encourage young women and pregnant teenagers who feel they have fallen from grace or ruined their lives to get back up and see that starting over is possible. No one is perfect and placing my imperfect life out on display is needed to ignite triumph, change, and bring out others' greatness. This book expresses how being flawed and learning from the past can be a blessing in disguise. At the end of the day, I did put my son up for adoption out of fear of my family, but my son has received a gift. A gift of happiness and stability that I could not give due to a number of reasons. This decision I will still always regret, but I do know that God makes no mistakes. My pain was meant to be shared and I do not believe God had me go through it in vain. If I was asked would I write a book about my story a year ago I would have denied it. I never wanted to be a writer or famous the spotlight never seemed to fit me. Unfortunately, I could not let go of this urge to help others like me. So, if I only reach one person, a handful, or the world with my book I can rest easy knowing lives are possibly being transformed.

There is a stigma that comes along with teenage pregnancy and adoption. This is another intention behind telling my story to possibly deter people from jumping to conclusions and understand facts. The idea of being pregnant at 16 was already a disgrace coming from the background I was raised in. However, based on my church and the black community giving a baby away to strangers (adoption) was unheard of and rare, to say the least. After I had my son, I was most definitely was looked down upon for doing the adoption. According to those around me that was taboo. The stereotypical idea in my community is that you either get an abortion, give the baby to someone else in your family to raise, or you keep it. Initially, I wanted to get an abortion for multiple reasons: one, I was young and afraid of my family finding out. Two, because I did not want to disappoint my family. Three, because I did not want to be judged for being pregnant at a young age. As scared as I was there was a part of me that would not allow me to let abortion be an option for me. I was stuck in limbo, I wanted to keep my baby since the damage was done, but I knew my family was completely against it. I hid my pregnancy from my family only telling my closest friends. When I was 5 months I broke down and confessed. My son's father was supposed to tell them with me, but he never showed up. This day was the beginning of what I call "war with myself." I was now at odds with whether I go along with what my family wanted, what was best for my baby, or what I wanted.

2
JUDGEMENT FROM THE WORLD

If being 16 and pregnant was not already a lot to accept, the thought of what people would say was even harder. I had only told two of my closest friends when I found out and that was difficult, but I knew they accepted me. Unfortunately, I knew that would not be the case for others which included my family and their friends. When I told my family they were livid, disappointed, and ashamed. I was told that because I was not married that the child, I was carrying was a mistake. I also was told that something had to be done, I could not keep this child. Initially, my father wanted me to have an abortion, but I was too far along. Then the next plan was to have me sent away to have the baby and come back without it. That one fell through after realizing that it would be a hassle. At the time I was staying with my grandmother and neither her nor my father could stand to look at me be pregnant. So, I was sent to stay with one of the elders from my church. I stayed there for the rest of the summer until school started.

I grew up in the church and so in my family's eyes having a baby out of wedlock was like committing murder. Everyone in my immediate family sat on a committee at the church. I also was in every activity you could think of at church, so this made everyone look bad. Of course, I knew I had gone against all of the morals and beliefs I grew up on, but at this point, none of that mattered. The weeks of me being at the elders' house were depressing and daunting. I had many conversations with her about my situation, and while it was uncomfortable and embarrassing, she made me still feel cared for. I was basically being held in limbo at her house until my family could decide their next course of action.

After three weeks went by, I received a phone call from my father. He told me since I sinned by breaking my vow to stay a virgin until marriage I should ask for forgiveness. When these words came through the phone my entire body went numb, for a second I was not following the conversation. I proceeded to ask him why? Then he cut me off and said, "It is what is best." As he continued talking, he referred to an event that took place months prior to me telling my family I was pregnant. It was a ceremony I was in where you openly tell everyone in the church you vow to keep your virginity. Because I had taken this vow, my father felt that I needed to openly ask the church if they would forgive me for getting pregnant. When I got off the phone I was in tears. I asked the elder whose house I was staying at, "why would he say that"? She was completely ok with it, thought it was a great idea along with my grandmother who was a deacon of the church.

The word "devastated" could not even describe how I felt more like disgusted. Disgusted with myself, my family, and the elder. All I could think about was how much more embarrassed I would be getting up in front of the entire church to cry my eyes out and struggle to not pass out. That night when I went to bed I tossed and turned cried, cried, and cried some more I felt like the scum of the earth. I know I had sinned in more than one way, but this was too much. That night I officially realized the dark side of the church I had always heard about growing up. The saints in the church that condemn others and forget that they themselves have sinned at one point too. So, a week went by and Wednesday night Bible study was in full swing. Before I got to church, I was instructed by my family and the elder to speak after praise and worship. The entire service was hell for me. The place I once reverenced and held in high esteem turned into what felt like a courtroom. My palms were sweaty, and I wanted to melt in my seat, like a snowman in summer. Finally, praise and worship had ended, and the spotlight was on me. When I walked to the pulpit my mouth was dry and my eyes started to water, everyone was starring some people were speculating about what was going on, but for the most part, no one knew anything. I looked over at my pastors and they looked at me with stern faces that's when I said in a trembling voice, "I am sorry please forgive me."

I ran off the pulpit into the bathroom with my face in my hands crying my eyes out. The more I tried to stop crying the more the tears flowed. Some of the other women who had children at a young age ran to my aide with hugs and questions. Some asked, "How far along are you?" Some said, "Are you going to keep it?" Some were upset that I was forced to be humiliated in front of everyone. I could not really talk; all I could do was cry. To be honest all I wanted to do was run away from everyone and everything that was going on. I could feel my belly flutter with every deep breath I took while trying to catch my breath. When I went back into the sanctuary my grandmother gave me this look of well done and went outside to call my father and let him know I did it. It took everything in me not to go outside and choke her from behind because that feeling of disgust came back over me. As much as my family felt they could not stand the sight of me, I felt the same towards them. My grandmother was only outside for 5 minutes and came back in to hand me the phone. My father was on the other end praising me for my public service announcement and said I am being a good example for other girls by doing what I did. I did not end up staying at church long after my announcement. I ended up going back home with the elder where I stayed up all night contemplating whether or not I should take my own life. I cried myself to sleep in hopes that that night was a dream. Unfortunately, I woke up the next day to the harsh reality that the world as I knew it was officially over.

The weeks went by and eventually, my father called the elder asking her to bring me home. It was a couple of weeks before school was to start and it was time for me to get prepared. Not just prepared for the classwork, but also the stares and comments from classmates.

3

SCHOOL RUMORS

My close friends, who were all of four people already knew what was going on and were more anxious than me to see what the future would hold that school year. I was six months pregnant by this time and clearly showing. The first week was rough between the side comments people were making while staring at my belly and the questions of who is the dad? At lunch everyone made me feel so uncomfortable laughing and pointing. My friends were trying to make me feel better by talking about other things, but it most definitely did not work. As we parted ways going to our different classes I felt like a complete outsider. I walked into all my classes with my head down and heart-pounding because all I could feel was the judgment from people's eyes. Unlike the students, my teachers were respectful and genuinely concerned; they could see the sadness and hurt all over my face. My child development teacher suggested I go see my guidance counselor and see what advice she could give me. After two weeks of going back and forth with myself about whether or not I should talk to my counselor, I went to her office. I was nervous, but I figured nothing worse could happen than what I was going through. When I got there, she was already privy to my situation based on the gossip she heard circulating through school, but she let me tell my own story. I stayed there for at least an hour talking, crying, and asking her what I should do. What should I do about my family pressuring me to give my child away? What should I do about finishing school? Lastly, I asked her why do I feel like by bringing this child into the world I am a failure? Surprisingly her response was simple, "It is all up to you".

I looked at her with devastation. I could not understand why she said that. I told her that I felt helpless and that things were not that easy. She said I can give you some information resources that could help, but there was not much she could do. She explained that by law she was limited and could not interfere unless it was life-threatening. We both could agree on the fact that my situation was not easy and the decisions I had to make moving forward would be difficult. The last two months of me being in school were frustrating, to say the least. I was being pulled in so many directions from friends to my teacher telling us what I should do. My child development teacher was adamant about me keeping my baby. telling me that there are other options and that I could go on to get my college degree with help. I told her I felt defeated and that after looking into the options her and the counselor suggested it was no way I could go that route. Those options would entail my family relinquishing all legal rights to me and my father was not going to do it. December 4th was my due date and it was drawing near. I stayed in school as long as possible, but I ended up in the hospital for the remainder of my pregnancy. At this point, I knew that my hiatus would strike up more

4

THE BIRTH

I ended up having to be in the hospital for a month due to complications. At certain times it felt like a breath of fresh air or a vacation from reality. The hospital was my new home and the staff made me feel like it was a home away from home. Unfortunately, the lost, afraid, young teenager was still very present. Each day that went by I was supposed to be closer to making a decision of what to do with my son. His father had left high school to get his G.E.D. and go to the army so he was no help. My family made it very clear that I could not return home with my baby. Then there was one of my mentors I had at the time. She came to the hospital one night after Bible study and brought me some food. She also started to tell me about this family that she knew who had children from a previous relationship but could not have any together. I asked her had they ever adopted before and she said no. I was hesitant and explained to her my stance on giving my son away. She acknowledged my concerns but suggested I think about it. Considering I was scared and felt powerless I knew that I did not want to leave my son at the hospital to be put in the system. At the time I let the fear of losing my family and what I knew drive me to make my decisions.

After 3 days of talking to my mentor, a social worker came into my room and asked to speak with me about my situation. I told her I was at a standstill and did not want to give him up, but my support system at home was nonexistent. She laid down four different folders in front of me that contained information on adoption agencies. I instantly broke down in tears. I hated myself for what I was about to do, but I felt it was the only way. After the social worker left, I picked up one of the folders and called the number. An agency counselor answered, and I began to inquire about the process. I told them I would call them back and I dialed my mentor's number. I asked her for the family's information so I could call them. The following day I reached out to them and they agreed to meet me that evening.

When they entered the room that night, I felt like I was interviewing them for a job. As I asked them questions about their life and their other kids my stomach was in knots. I felt like I was going to lose it, I had to stop 20 minutes into the visit and ask them to leave. I had had enough for the day it was too overwhelming to think about. I asked the nurses if they could push me around to get out of the room and they did. That trip around the hospital helped me go to sleep that night, but I knew the next day I had to face life again. I spoke with the agency the following morning and told them I had found a couple I wanted to adopt my son. They asked me was I sure I did not want to go with any of their families and I assured them I was ok with my decision. They reached out to the couple and the agency started their process. Two weeks went by and I was still having complications. My doctor felt that I was close enough to my due date where they could take the baby. So, on November 17, 2008, I gave birth to my beautiful baby boy.

The nurses were awesome. I could not have a better group of women take care of me that day. At a time where I was supposed to be excited about bringing life into the world, everyone wanted to control the situation. The nurses asked who I wanted to go with me into surgery. I elected to go back by myself with one of my favorite nurses. The adoptive parents and my dad were livid, but this was strictly my moment. My father was adamant about telling the doctor in a life-threatening situation to save me and let my son die. Despite his harsh and disturbing comments, the medical staff kept their professionalism and kept me calm going into surgery. I am not exactly sure how long the C-section took but I know when they woke me up, I saw my precious baby boy. I was in the hospital for five short days after giving birth. I tried to stretch them out as long as possible—the doctor gave me an extra day so I could spend it with my son.

Those four days were bittersweet, and I can say that the first and the last days were hardest. The first day Elijah's soon to be new family swarmed my hospital room. Everyone wanted to shower him with kisses and words of adornment. I, on the other hand, wanted to run away with him and never turn back. All I could think about was what I was about to do in a couple of days. Giving this precious baby away made me feel like the scum of the earth like I did not deserve to carry him in my womb. Over the next two days, I held him and watched him sleep as much as I could. My father visited me, and he tried every effort to avoid seeing him: whether that be going in the opposite direction to avoid walking past the nursery or avoid the nurse bringing him to my room. I really was not in the mood to see him or hear his voice. I could not understand how he could come to see me after giving me the ultimatum to leave my family or my son behind. He did not stay long as he could tell he was not wanted by my body language.

The fourth day grew near and morning came. I spent as much time as I could with him in between the nurses taking him to the nursery. Later that evening his new parents came in to take him home and I was heartbroken. As they walked out of the door and down the hall with him in the car seat, I went ballistic. I started screaming and crying out please do not take my baby. It took 3 nurses to get me under control and once I was, reality set in that he was no longer my baby. The fifth day it was time for me to return back home to hell on earth as I saw it. Before I left my doctor came and saw me and he told me my story was one of the rarest and saddest he had witnessed, but he believed I would be ok. My nurses surprised me and brought me a baby bag full of baby stuff from my son. Everything from his shirts they changed in the nursery to his hats, pacifiers, and even a piece of his hair.

They treated me as if I was still a mother and they all cried with me and wished me the best. Everyone who had come in contact with me at the hospital knew how hard this was and made me feel special and important even though all I wanted to do was be nonexistent. This was a time in my life I will forever cherish thanks to the staff at St. Mary's Hospital in Richmond, Va.

5

OPEN OR CLOSED

When I was faced with my limited options from my father to choose adoption or leaving my baby at the hospital to go into foster care, I obviously chose adoption. Even though I chose that I was not well informed on what that truly meant other than losing all parental control. A month after leaving the hospital I was required by the agency to come to their office and sign paperwork. I was told by the caseworker that I would need to make a decision on if the adoption would be open or closed.

Now I was under the impression that for it to be open it meant the adoptive family would allow me to visit and send updates, and of course, closed would mean no contact moving forward. As the caseworker went on to explain the difference, I learned that my assumption was wrong.

According to the agency, an open adoption pertains to the paperwork involved. Stating that I would like for Elijah to have access to the adoption records when he is 18 in his attempt to find out information about me. A closed adoption would mean that I would want those records to stay sealed. This was a no brainer for me. I knew that I would one day want him to be able to find me in case his adoptive parents did not tell him. So, I expressed that an open adoption would make me feel like I was getting something, even a small piece of hope out of this grim situation. It did cause me to question whether or not he would want to find me when he grew up. Or would I be possibly doing him a favor by sparing him emotional heartache if I stayed a mystery? Despite those thoughts, I stuck with my decision.

From the beginning of this journey up until now the forgiveness process has taken many unexpected turns. Making choices like the open or closed adoption and not standing up for how I really felt every second of this time in my life I grapple with why I went through with everything. In my opinion, forgiveness is one of the hardest things to do. This is something I constantly go back and forth with myself about. It has been 10 years since I started this journey, but I have to forgive myself daily. Now I know that seems strange because for most of my life I have been told once you forgive you move on. While that might sound easy, the task seems impossible. My mind says you did the right thing and he is better off where he is. My heart holds regret and grieves the separation. With these two feelings combined, I do not think forgiveness has completely happened for me yet.

I would like to forgive myself for walking away from my son when I could have fought harder to keep him. I also would like to forgive myself for allowing others to make me believe I could not be successful, because I made a mistake. The mistake not being my son but getting pregnant before marriage. Some days I feel like I have let go and forgiven myself. The pain that I felt from day one still creeps in my heart when I am quiet and reflecting on life. Despite all of my feelings whether positive or negative, I have to remind myself daily that God has forgiven me and there is no magic formula that can rush my healing.

Then there is forgiving those in my life that did not properly support me through the process. This is also hard because they judged without remembering that they too are not perfect. From the people I looked up to in the church to my immediate family, their actions left a scar that aches when I have flashbacks from that time in my life. A part of me has made peace with what they did because I know they have to answer for their actions. On the other hand, I am still hurt. I can say overall that the hatred that festered in my heart has diminished. I no longer wish for their demise, but now I pray that they reconcile with God.

6

GRIEVING SEPERATION

After I had Elijah and left the hospital it was time to go back to hell as I knew it. I was healing from surgery, but my emotional and mental state were far from being healed. As the weeks went by my family was continuing on with their normal routines without any regard for my feelings. My father and I were not really on speaking terms and as far as I was concerned, he could drop dead and I would not care. When we did speak, I would answer with one-word answers. There were days I felt like I was worthless and nights I wished were my last. Needless to say, I was depressed and grieving the loss of my baby. Of course, he was still naturally living— but living without me.

The thoughts rushed through my head constantly: "How could I let this happen?"; "Why did I ruin my son's life by leaving him?" I tried to wish the hurt away, pray it away, and cry it away. Unfortunately, there was no easy way out of that pain. I ended up going to counseling two different times. The first time was with the adoption agency which was not that great. The counselor told me that all of my feelings were normal, and I would be fine with time. She was more so trying to push her agenda of making sure I did not pull out of the adoption process more than help me through my time of grieving. The second counseling session was with an outside counselor who made me cry more than I was before. Not because she was being harsh or rude, but because she made me confront my true demon. That demon was standing up for what I wanted and not what others around me wanted. I expressed to her, of course, I hated myself for my decision, but I felt my hands were tied. She told me that no matter what decision I made it would be hard and I have to stand in my own truth. I got a lot of my chest in that session, but I still had to return home where her philosophy was not welcomed.

Days at home were like fighting a battle I had never seen or heard of before. At times I said to myself maybe I should ask my doctor for medication to help with my depression, but I could not bring myself to do it. I told myself that I was not going to let this situation defeat me, even though my heart broke over and over again daily.

One day I could not take it anymore and I called the lawyer of the family that had him and told them I want to pull out of the adoption. All hell broke loose after that phone call. The couple called my father furious at the news. When I got home,

everyone pounced on me at once. My stepmother greeted me at

the door cursing me out asking me how dare I change my mind.

My father came right behind her and went on ranting the same

way. He made me sit down and listen to my stepmother's uncle

tell me about young single mothers he has dealt with in his line

of work. He claimed if I got my son and was in a group home

how bad things would be, and I would not survive. My

grandmother came in the middle of the lecture and tried to come

across the room and choke me. My feelings were beyond hurt by

their comments and I wanted to run away. And that is exactly

what ended up happening. I was told by my father that if I

wanted my baby back, I had to leave his house and that I was no

longer considered a part of his family. With one duffle bag full of

clothes and the baby bag I got from the hospital I started walking

to my best friend's house. I ended up getting a ride there and

when I got there, I called the police. I told them what happened, and they reassured me that my dad could not put me out since I was a minor. I pleaded with the officer that I did not want to go back, because they were crazy; but he told me I had to. He called my father and explained to him what he told me and that what he did was illegal. I told the officer I did not want to go home that night and my friend's mom let me stay. I was devastated to say the least. How could being kicked out from the place I hated be illegal? When I got to school the next day my guidance counselor called me to the office and told me my father was on the phone. He told me that I was being ridiculous and needed to come home after school. I reluctantly went home that evening and wanted to quickly turn back around and run out. I felt lonely and helpless and was convinced by my family that I was better off giving up trying to be a mom and move on.

My father told me that if I attempted to run away again that he would call the police to come get me for going against him, painting me out to be a rebellious uncontrollable minor. Months went by and the hate towards myself and my father grew stronger. All I wanted was to escape my life by death or trade places with someone. Regardless of how I felt I knew that life would move on and there was nothing I could do the family with my son had a lawyer and I did not nor did I have a good support system. The only thing I could tell myself was to keep pushing through my pain and there were brighter days to come. So, from that day forward I devised a plan to finish high school and move out away from my family.

7

THE FINAL GOODBYE

A month after my failed attempt to pull out of the adoption it was time to go to court. On this particular day, I was supposed to be relinquishing my parental rights to my baby boy. When I woke up that morning, I felt like I was going on trial for some heinous crime. Before my grandmother and I left to go to court my father called a "family meeting" in the living room. He told me that he was sending my grandmother with me to make sure I go through with giving up my rights. He also made it clear that if I was to deviate from the plans when I got home there would be repercussions. As we pulled out of the driveway my grandmother talked to me as if it was a normal day. She talked about people at church, the weather, etc.

Much like my grandmother, my father was also emotionally disconnected from the events that happened that day. He told me that he could not understand why I was sad about the adoption. He said that if I was not physically around my baby I should not be affected. I stared at him in awe because he clearly had no clue how ignorant his comment sounded. The out of sight out of mind mentality was expected to be second nature to me since it was an adopted practice by everyone in my household. Sadly, I was affected and hurt, because I carried that baby in my womb through all the stress I had to endure. He felt my every move, heard me cry and talk to him every night. We had a bond before I met him on the day, I gave birth. His being away from me was undoubtedly the hardest thing I have been through in my life. Some days I can admit to almost accepting my father's ideology because the regret felt so strong. At the end of the day when I sit back and reevaluate my deepest thoughts and feelings, I know that I can never forget my son.

8

VISITATION

For the first three years of Elijah's life, I did not see him; I only received pictures. During that time frame, I was trying to put the pieces of my life together after having him. I was preparing for college and moving out of my father's house into my godparent's home. Even after I moved out and left to go to school, I still found it hard and wanted to physically see him. I was carrying around so much sadness and regret that I did not feel worthy to be in his presence. I also felt like there was not any purpose of wanting to visit with him since he was a baby and would not care. Lastly, in the back of my mind, I felt like I was meaningless in his life because he had new parents and I did not fit in the family dynamic.

After he turned five, I decided to let go of my fears and negative thoughts and asked if I could see him. By this time, I had my oldest daughter and I had been living in Georgia. Her dad and I had visitation set up where he would get her for the summer, and I would pick her up from Virginia when it was over. So, I figured me coming back to pick up my daughter would be a great time to see Elijah. I reached out to his adoptive mother and asked when a good day would be to meet. She was shocked that I asked since I had been distant for a couple of years, but she agreed to meet with me. I also asked her would it be okay if I brought my daughter and she also agreed to that. The first meeting was at Chick-fil-a which at the time was his favorite restaurant. Initially, I was scared and anxious and did not know what I was going to say or what to expect. I got there before them and went inside to order some food. As my daughter and I waited at the table they walked in and I almost passed out. Prior to coming, I had prayed that I would be strong and not break down and cry.

Unfortunately, all of that went out of the window and I did the complete opposite. I could not believe how big he was and that he looked just like me. After I composed myself, I gave him a hug and asked him how he was doing. He looked confused and I could tell he felt uncomfortable, so he asked if he could go play in the indoor playground with my daughter. They both went to go play and surprisingly he hit it off with his sister. Of course, neither knew of each other nor knew they were related, but they took to each other as if they did. He was protective of her the entire time they played and made sure she did not fall or hurt herself. His adoptive parents and I were both amazed at the connection and neither of us interfered, we let them continue to play. We took pictures and wrapped up the hour-long visit. When I got in my car, I sat there for ten minutes and wept again. I could not believe I finally saw him and visited with him. I was proud of myself because I had all of these dreams that maybe when I saw him, I would run out of the room. I also dreamt that I would throw up from being so nervous about seeing him. Thankfully none of the above happened and I made through it in one piece. After this, I promised myself that when I came into town, I would attempt to set up a visit with him.

Since then I have been visiting with him every year for the past five years. Each year things become more complicated because he does not understand why we meet. He looks at me like he wants to ask me why, but his adoptive mom reassures him that I am a friend of the family then he runs off to go play. Now that he is older, we can have some conversation about things that interest him. His attention span is very short, but

40

he will talk for about 10 minutes at the most. We talk about school, the sports that he plays, his adoptive siblings, and his favorite action figures. I am in amazement when I listen to him talk and his body language, he is very mature. After he and I talk his mother talks to me about his day to day activities and his growth overall. Sometimes the conversation between her and I can get personal very quickly. For example, there was a visit in summer 2017 where the word personal was an understatement to describe not just the conversation, but the entire 2 hours I was there. First of all, it was already awkward because I had brought both of my daughters. I did that only at her request because she wanted them to take pictures with Elijah. Normally I would have left them at home because I feel that it would complicate things. Especially since my oldest daughter found out about her brother without me knowing through a relative. We decided to meet at McDonald's that had a playhouse for the kids to play but my girls were far from interested in playing. Before we walked in, I told Zariah that we were going to meet someone that I knew and to be quiet the entire time. She agreed and we walked into the restaurant. When we sat down, we greeted Elijah, his adoptive mother, and her 2-year-old daughter. Elijah and I did our usual talk then he gave me a hug and went to go play. I tried to encourage Zariah and to do the same, but she was stiff as a board barely breathing and looking scared. I told her it was okay that she could calm down and breathe. She did relax but was still adamant about staying at the table with me and her sister. His mother had a bewildered look on her face, and I explained to her that I told her not to talk. I also explained to her that Zariah was aware that Elijah was her brother but was told not to mention it. So, after all of that, she proceeded to tell me that she and her husband were divorced and had been for quite some time. She also told me that since their separation her ex-husband did not want to tell Elijah he was adopted, nor did he want us to continue our visits. Before I could process the information, I was hearing she proceeded to tell me that Elijah was never legally adopted. I was obviously shocked to hear of the separation, but more shocked about the latter statement. My heart sank into my stomach and completely baffled I looked at her in disbelief.

For some reason, things were not registering to me and I started asking a host of questions. The first was why not? With her eyes watering she explained that because of her ex's criminal background the agency stopped the process. She also said that when she wanted to get a lawyer and do it directly through the court he objected. The second was how long had they known they could not adopt him? Her response was in the earlier part of 2009. My last question was what was his issue with me? And she told me that he is afraid that Elijah would not love him anymore. She also said that he was afraid I would try to take him away from them. I expressed to her while I understand his concerns that I am not that type of person and I would not take him away from everything he knows. She attempted to apologize for his actions and explain that she does not feel the same way. I told her I appreciated her candidness and wrapped up the visit and left.

Needless to say, I was overwhelmed with emotion and wanted to forget everything that happened that day. Lamentably I could not ignore her voice playing in my head from when she was telling me everything. On one hand, I was livid and on the other, I felt desolate. I wanted to cry, but the tears would not fall. All I could do was feel this weight on my chest of regret and heartbreak. How could I have been so stupid to trust them? How could I have allowed myself to be brainwashed into thinking these people were a better fit for my son than me? Regardless of what I thought the damage had already been done my legal rights were terminated.

9

COLLEGE BREAKDOWN

After everything that happened with giving my son away, I had no desire to be around my father. In 2010, my senior year of high school, I moved out of his house and in with my godparents. I graduated and attended a college that Fall in hopes of turning over a new leaf and never looking back at my past. Little did I know my past was going to alter my future more than I could fathom. When I got to college the first couple of weeks were bittersweet I was still adjusting to being away from home and trying to make new friends. As the weeks continued to pass, I went through a lot of ups and downs with my roommates and tried to stay on top of my grades. As if I was not already an emotional wreck, I found myself getting sad and crying randomly almost every day.

At first, I thought it was the pressure from the new environment and tried ignoring my feelings. Convincing myself I was being weak and overdramatic. Then one night I completely broke down in my dorm room. My roommate walked in on me crying my eyes out screaming. She kept asking what was wrong. I would not answer her. She ran out to get one of our friends and they ran in the room trying to console me. She tried to calm me down and talk, but I ran out of the room and walked the campus for an hour. I texted my roommate and told her that I would explain later and that I would be okay. While I walked the campus that night, I realized I was depressed from what happened with Elijah. I also called my best friend when I was outside walking and told her I did not think I was strong enough to live with myself knowing that I gave my baby away. She told me to not beat myself up because my choices were limited, but in my heart what she said did not ease my pain. I walked back to my dorm and apologized to my roommate for scarring her. While she was privy to my son's adoption, she did not know I was hurting in silence. She gave me a hug and told me if I needed to talk, she was always there.

While I appreciated her thoughtful words, I knew that I needed to talk to a professional. I went to the school counselor and set up my first appointment. The following day we met and as soon as she asked me what I wanted to talk about I broke out in tears. After I collected myself, I explained that I was having a hard time dealing with my son's adoption. I continued to give her details of my story and she said she was speechless.

When the session was over, we agreed to meet once a week. Each session brought me to the realization that I was not only depressed but running away from the truth. The truth that I hated myself for not fighting harder to keep my son. I allowed my family to intimidate me and convince me that if I did not give up my baby I would one not be successful and that they would disown me. At a time in my life when I was supposed to be happy and excited to start a new chapter called college, I was devastated. The counselor helped me see that I had to stop living in fear of my family and teach myself that I am, I can, and will be great. This particular time in my life was say the least rough. For the two semesters I was at school I tried to not think about my past and pain, but when I closed my eyes trying to sleep and being alone made it harder. I eventually made friends and had a lot of good memories, but I always felt that hole in my heart.

10

HAVING OTHER CHILDREN

In 2012, I had my oldest daughter Zariah and in 2016 I had

my youngest daughter Harmoni. Now back in 2008 when I had

my son, I could never imagine having any more children. The

idea made me sick to my stomach because I thought how could

I ever love anyone else more than him? At the time I also felt

like in a way I would be betraying him because I kept other kids

and not him. When I conceived Zariah, I was happy and

nervous, because I was going to raise this child. It might sound normal but for me, I was lost. I had been pregnant before but keeping the child was a new ball game.

The entire 9 months were full of anxiety and pressure that I put on myself because I did not think I could love her enough. After she was born, I went through postpartum depression. One reason was that she cried all the time, but also because I felt I was a bad mother. I say a bad mom because I kept her and not my son. A lot of nights in the first few months of her life I questioned myself, was I worthy to be her mother. Once she turned 6 months, I started to fall in love with the fact that I was fortunate to be her mother. When I got pregnant with her my circumstances were by far perfect, but I realized I was blessed to have her. Becoming pregnant at 19 with Zariah was still very young to be a mom especially since I was in college when it happened. That is what led me to feel that things were not that much better from being pregnant at 16 to 19. I still was learning a lot about myself and hurting from the situation with my son.

In my mind life was supposed to look and feel different when I had a second chance to be a mother. I should have been married, graduated from school, have a great career, and be stable. At this point I found myself about to embark on a journey that was toilsome and unlike anything I had ever experienced. My relationship with Zariah's father did not last, and I learned how much stronger I was going to have to be by deciding to raise her as a single mother. Four years later I had Harmoni. When I got pregnant this last time it was unexpected also, but I knew she would be the last of the clan. While I dealt with less anxiety, I still felt like I was not worthy to carry and have another child. Throughout this pregnancy, I worked the entire time grinding to prepare for her arrival. I also grinded so hard, because deep down I had something to prove. To prove to myself that I was not a failure, because I was pregnant. To also prove that I could be "wonder woman" self-sufficient and have a baby. This was important to me because I was told I could not be successful because I made a mistake. Or I could not overcome obstacles, because I was not capable or competent. Now I can honestly say that after having my daughter's things have not been easy breezy. The highs and lows of parenting have some days stopped me in my tracks and made me question why did I keep them? There are other days I also think maybe my son got the better life because he does not have to see me struggle.

Fortunately, after a long day of working my two jobs, doing homework with my daughter, cooking, and putting girls to bed I count my blessings. I count them because things could be worse regardless of the circumstances with all of my children. I have had to first accept myself and flaws. Secondly, I have had to forgive myself for not doing life the way I thought it should have been done when I had each of my kids. By doing this I have come to terms with the idea that one day all of my children will be together and know each other. My oldest daughter Zariah found out about her brother through a relative that did not consult me before doing it. She has asked about him and I confirmed that she, in fact, does have a brother, but I am withholding details. I am waiting until the adoptive parents tell Elijah he is adopted. I figure there is no use in talking about this with her if she cannot talk to him. With that said I am continuously preparing myself for this unforgettable event and pray that I give them all the gift of transparency, honesty, and love.

11

THE ANXIETY OVER REJECTION

I am 26 now and there is a question I ask myself daily. Will

Elijah accept me? Acceptance for me includes my truth, my

other kids, and the love I want to give him. I always tell my

immediate family that when he comes to me with questions

about the adoption or anything, I will be transparent. I mean

that with everything in me, but I am afraid where that may lead.

He might hate me or might be understanding. Either way, it is up to him to open himself up to the emotions he will inherit with the truth. When I think about the future, I have mixed feelings. On one side I long for the day to come when he can acknowledge me as his mother. On the other side, I want to crawl under a rock, because I don't want him to be hurt.

I can personally relate to having some of the feelings he might feel when he finds out. I say that with full confidence because my mother left me to be raised by my grandparents. I always wondered why she left and never returned. I heard stories from family, but never her story out of her mouth. When I became an adult, I found her and asked everything I could think of. From, "Why did you leave?" to "Did you want to get me back?" She didn't want to talk about anything. For a while, I hated her. I even wished for her demise, but I had to realize she was broken too. From then on, I promised myself if there was any gift, I could give my son it would be answers.

When my mother felt the need to withhold answers, I felt like I was not good enough to hear them. If nothing else, it could have been closure and insight for me. The insight I need to approach my son and deal with the regret I carry in my heart for leaving him.

I pray daily that God gives me the strength and words to say when I tell him my side of the truth. I say my side because everyone involved in my journey has a truth that contributed to my son's adoption. My dad, my grandmother, his biological father, and his adopted family. All I choose to tell Elijah is mine. A part of his curiosity will be to ask about other people involved, why they let it happen and what role they played. I know that there is a possibility he will be upset if I do not tell him, and I know he might not want to talk anymore. I would never want to hurt him more or have him walk out of my life because he feels I am withholding things. I hope he will understand that I want him to reach out to the other people so they can speak for themselves. Everyone involved knows this day will come and he deserves to hear everyone's side individually. We all make decisions in our lives and if those decisions affect the wellbeing of others when confronted with questions, we should be confident in our answers. No one is perfect—especially me— and, I hope he can take that into consideration while he is contemplating our future as mother and son.

Part II

12

FROM TRAGEDY TO NEW BEGINNINGS

It is amazing how God brings life full circle to show us how his plans and our plans are different. I could have never anticipated how my life was going to be forever changed when 2019 began. Of course, I was writing this book and I was confident that by February I would be finished and moving on to my next venture. Unfortunately, God decided that he needed to do a course correction on my journey.

In the first week of January, I picked up Zariah from her father after she had visited with him for the Christmas break.

While I was in Virginia, I decided to reach out to Elijah's adoptive mother to set up a visit. She agreed and everything to my knowledge seemed to be fine. The next day I reached out to her and she explained there was not going to be a visit. She explained that her ex-husband had Elijah and did not want him to see me. I was very frustrated because I had bought a gift to give him and just wanted to lay my eyes on him. I was also livid because I felt that his dad had something against me and was finding every excuse to keep our visits from happening. Ever since their divorce, he was against Elijah having any connection with me. He allowed his insecurities to overshadow the bigger picture and was choosing to be spiteful. I was more than offended not only from the rejection but also because I had not done anything wrong. I talked to the adoptive mother expressing my frustration and explained I would try again the next time I was due to return to Virginia for my daughter. Unfortunately, an unforeseen event brought me back to

Virginia sooner than expected, and it would change everything.

13

TURNING OF A TIDE

Two weeks after returning to Georgia I received a phone call that Zariah's father was killed. My world stopped and nothing else mattered. It took everything out of me to tell my 6-year-old the devastating news. All I kept thinking was I just left Virginia! How, why, what is next? Were the questions that kept swarming my mind. The following week me, my girls, and aunt were on the road back to VA for the funeral. Halfway through the drive I turned to my aunt and told her I wanted to reach back out to Elijah's mother. She gave me a look and asked why? I expressed to her that despite the rejection to see him weeks before I wanted to try seeing him again. Her response was to follow my heart and pray for a positive outcome.

I sent a text to his mom and explained to her that I was on my way back to VA for a funeral and that I would like to see Elijah. She replied instantly, explaining to me that it was ironic I was coming back that particular week because she had been trying to find a way to tell Elijah he was adopted that week too. She also said that she did not mind us meeting and asked if I wanted to do it considering the circumstances I was coming back home for? My jaw dropped and I was in shock. I read the text to my aunt and we both sat in silence for a moment trying to grasp what I had read. She asked me how I felt and was I ready for him to meet me as his biological mother. My eyes started to tear up and I explained that I had been waiting for this moment for 10 years, but I was nervous. Nervous about rejection, the questions he would ask, and what if my answers were not good enough.

It was Thursday when I arrived in town and I told his mom that Friday we could do it since I was leaving Saturday. I also told her that I understood that at that particular time things were hectic, and it was a sad occasion, but I would not miss this for anything. As I had learned from past experiences that circumstances and people change their minds quickly so if I would have hesitated or passed up the chance it probably would not have happened. So, with the rest of the drive to VA ahead of us, Zariah's dad's wake, meeting with Elijah, and the funeral I was stressed, to say the least. All I kept thinking was am I crazy or dreaming? How am I going to handle all of this in one weekend all while I am sick with later what I found out was pneumonia? I did not have a clue, but I was about to find out.

We arrived at the hotel Thursday evening, tired, and mentally drained. After settling in we unpacked and called it a night. Friday came, I took my daughter to her grandparent's house and then to the wake. As if that was not emotionally draining in itself, I dropped Zariah off back at the hotel and went to meet Elijah. On the drive to the restaurant where we agreed to meet my entire body felt numb. I kept replaying in my head all the times I prayed for this day was to come. I never could have imagined it would be under those circumstances, but if that was it so be it. I pulled up to the restaurant and parked the car with my hands trembling holding the steering wheel. I took a deep breath and asked God to guide my words and help me be as honest as possible. I stepped out of the car, walked into the restaurant and was greeted at the door by Elijah. The huge smile on his face surprised me but also was a relief for me. He hugged me really tight and grabbed my hand to take me to the table his mother was sitting at. She told me that he wanted to get ice cream and spend alone time with me. I agreed and took him across the street to the ice cream shop.

From the time he hopped in the car to the time we sat down to eat our ice cream he kept smiling and staring at me. I can admit I was kind of shy myself and his unexpected reaction to being around me made me nervous. We sat down at the table and paused for 3 minutes until I broke the ice by asking him how did he feel? He replied that he was happy and upset at the same time. He also explained that he was happy to know the truth, but upset it took so long for his parents to tell him. Around age 8 he said he had a dream that God told him he had parents somewhere else, but he dismissed it because that could not be true. Then after he found out that it was true, he said he was happy to know he was not crazy. I laughed and assured him he was far from crazy and that God has his way of preparing us for things unforeseen to us.

Finally, the moment I had been waiting for presented itself the questions of why. Elijah took a deep breath and proceeded to ask me would I get mad if he asked me questions? I said of course not, I am ready, ask away. First, he asked why I gave him away? I explained that I was young, with no job or money, and not a great support system at home. My parents felt that it was the best for both of us. He tilted his head to the side and said hold on your parents are my grandparents', right? So, if that is the case why would they want us separated? With my heart feeling like it had dropped to my stomach, I replied by saying that sometimes parents think that the decisions they are making at the time are in their child's best interest. By doing this they sometimes lose sight of what is important and that their decisions could turn out to be bad later.

His next question was how did I feel when I had to give him to his parents? At this point, I had a knot in my throat with my legs shaking trying to keep myself from crying. This question amongst all of them was the hardest to answer; not because I was ashamed or afraid to talk about it, but because I had to relive that devastating moment in my life. I told him that it was one of the hardest things I have ever had to do, and I felt like my heart was being ripped out my chest. He could see the pain in my eyes and told me he did not mean to make me upset. He grabbed my hand on the table and said if I am ten then that means we have been separated for 10 years? I shook my head yes and apologized to him for leaving him when I should have stayed. He kept shocking me with his level of maturity because after that he told me he was not mad at me and he loved me. I could not believe what I was hearing. For ten years I feared he would hate me, but I reality he didn't. He continued to piece together how many siblings he had from me and how excited he was to have more people to love. I wrapped up our ice cream date with questions about how he was doing in school and how he liked his parents? He talked about his favorite subjects and explained he liked them, but his parents always fought about him and he didn't like that.

We left and went to go meet his mom across the street at

McDonald's. While we waited on her to meet us, he asked me why didn't his biological dad come to see him? I told him it was a lot going on and his schedule wouldn't allow him to come. I offered to call him so he could speak to him on the phone and he answered on the first ring. Elijah's eyes lit up when he heard his voice. His dad did not expect the call either, so when I told him what was going on, he was speechless. I told Elijah he could ask him whatever he wanted, and he did exactly that. He asked him everything from his favorite sport to what subject was he good at in school. At a certain point in the conversation, they both paused, and Elijah was smiling ear to ear while I could hear his dad doing the same. I laughed thinking to myself I am grateful that his reaction to this entire evening was positive. They wrapped up the phone call and we headed inside to find his mom.

We all sat down and she asked Elijah did he have any questions for either one of us while we were all together? He looked up at her and asked why didn't you tell me sooner? Her eyes were filled with tears while she tried to compose herself. She replied that she did not know how or when was best to tell him. She also said that his dad didn't want him to know so she tried to follow his lead. He expressed to her that he was happy to have met me and that he knew he was different; he just could not put his finger on it.

She asked how Zariah was handling the death of her dad and we talked for a few minutes about it. After that, we all got ourselves together to leave. Before we left Elijah ran up to me and gave me a huge hug. While we hugged, he looked up at me and told me he loved me, missed me, and that it was ok to cry. Obviously, by this time my face was full of tears not wanting to let him go, but I knew we had to go back to our separate lives. The next day I took the girls to meet Elijah. Zariah had been around him before but did not know he was her brother. Harmoni and Elijah had never met before. This particular meeting was bittersweet especially for Zariah and me, because of the loss we both had to accept. So, Zariah obviously was not thrilled to see him, but I could tell she was paying close attention to him. He tried to comfort her, apologizing to her for what happened to her dad. On the other hand, it was a pivotal moment in our lives since we lost her dad, but she gained a brother and I gained a son in a sense. Harmoni was not old enough to appreciate what was happening, but years from now I know she will. After we left visiting him the girls, my aunt, and I got on the road to return to Georgia. Part of the trip back was somber in a sense because I closed a chapter of my life when I said goodbye to Zariah's dad. It also was a relieving feeling that lingered in my spirit knowing my son finally knew the truth.

MAYA THOMAS

14

LIFE AFTER THE BIG REVEAL

7 months after Elijah and I met for the first time as mother and son, my so-called adoption journey took a turn for the worst. One day I called to check on him and I was informed that he was not doing well. He not only was not doing well in school, but his behavior had also spiraled out of control. His mom thought it might be due to her and her ex's separation. Besides that, a lot of other things had transpired including her ex being manipulative in how he handled visitation with Elijah. He also was furious about him finding out about me and was

pushing the issue that he was not to see me or communicate with me every again. After hearing all of this I was confident that all of these things contributed to him acting out. When it all set in that my child was unhappy and seemed to have been for a while my heart sunk.

For weeks after that phone call, my heart continued to break over and over again. I questioned how could that joyous moment that started my 2019 off come down to this? Also, how could I have let this happen? Even though I was forced to give my son away I had told myself for so many years he was better off. In my heart of hearts, I grappled with going through with the adoption and how I knew it was a mistake. Now after knowing everything that had been happening it was confirmation that it was. Unfortunately, reality set in again that there was nothing I could do to come to my baby boy's aide.

The painful truth was that at 16 I made an irreversible decision when I terminated all of my rights. Which in turn means that I have to watch by the sidelines and pray that he comes out of all of this mentally and emotionally stable.

15

CAUTIONARY TALE

As I have stated earlier in my story when I started this journey, I was young, afraid, uneducated about all of my options. My support group was not much of a support and I had no one to thoroughly explain the repercussions of giving my son away. Not only did I get shortchanged out of thinking there would be an adoption, but I also made a permanent decision that legally I cannot reverse. When I gave him away along with that came relinquishing all my parental rights to him. So, regardless of what happens moving forward legally I cannot do anything. They have sole custody and I am left to watch everything unfold. Like myself and others who have gone the adoption route, we were told everything would be great and the child would live a more fulfilling life. Unfortunately, you don't get the other talk about when it is not a good fit and things do not go as planned. I understand while some might try, the reality is no one knows what the future holds and bad things happen no matter what you do; but being well informed and confident about choices makes a difference. Having your voice heard and counted as a meaningful one also matters.

To those young girls who will and who are in my shoes be in the know and do what is best for you and your baby. Whatever your decision is let it be yours and yours alone. Remember that it takes a strong woman to step up and be a mother that provides and raises a child. It also takes a strong woman to let go and give a child to someone who can and will give them a better life. Do not allow anyone to diminish your light and make you feel unworthy because you became pregnant and life has taken a detour. To the women who have gone through what I have experienced keep your head up and know that healing and restoration takes time. Our walk through this process does not make us weak or incompetent but has made us even stronger than we thought we were.

Made in the USA
Columbia, SC
11 February 2021